MW01155586

EYE TO EYE WITH DOGS

ALASKAN MALAMUTES

Lynn M. Stone

Rourke
Publishing LLC
Vero Beach, Florida 32964

www.rourkepublishing.com

PHOTO CREDITS: All photos © Lynn M. Stone

Title page: *A malamute finds a cool couch in a snowdrift.*

Acknowledgments: For their help in the preparation of this book, the author thanks Robin Haggard, Cindy Hocking, Sharon and Larry Kalous, Jim Kuehl, Reva Reinelt, Angelique Roberts-Hertz, Nancy and Bob Russell, and Cheena Villano.

Editor: Frank Sloan

Cover and page design by Nicola Stratford

Library of Congress Cataloging-in-Publication Data

Stone, Lynn M.
  Alaskan malamutes / Lynn M. Stone.
     p. cm. -- (Eye to eye with dogs II)
  Includes bibliographical references and index.
  ISBN 1-59515-290-3 (hardcover)
  1. Alaskan Malamute--Juvenile literature. I. Title. II. Series: Stone, Lynn M.
Eye to eye with dogs II.
  SF429.A67S76 2004
  636.73--dc22
                                                          2004008021

Printed in the USA

CG/CG

Table of Contents

The malamute's thick fur makes a warm body. A wet tongue makes a warm nose.

The Alaskan Malamute

The original **ancestor** of all dogs was the wolf. The Alaskan malamute, however, is one of the few dogs that still *looks* like a wolf. Pat a malamute and it almost feels like a wolf. That's because it has long "guard" hairs and a woolly undercoat. Like the wolf's coat, the malamute's coat offers plenty of protection from the cold.

ALASKAN MALAMUTE FACTS

Weight: 75-85 pounds
(34-39 kilograms)
Height: 23-25 inches
(59-64 centimeters)
Country of Origin:
United States(Alaska)
Life Span: 10-12 years

Don't be fooled by the malamute's wolfish look. The malamute has been part of human families for hundreds of years. They are much more relaxed than wolves or even their Siberian husky cousins.

The Siberian husky is a faster, smaller Arctic dog than the Alaskan malamute.

Wolf or dog? Narrow muzzle, ears more closely set, and yellow eyes reveal the malamute's ancestor, the wolf.

Malamutes are extremely strong, rugged dogs. Like other "spitz-type" **breeds**, they were first developed in the cold of the Far North. All the spitz breeds tend to have thick coats, curly tails, and extra strength for their size.

Malamutes are placed in the working dog group. They were developed to hunt large animals, haul freight, and pull sleds.

Romping in deep snow is a winter party for a fun-loving malamute.

The leader of a malamute sled team stops to watch something on the trail ahead.

Many malamutes still pull sleds or compete in weight pulls. Many other malamutes are kept simply as good-natured family companions or show dogs.

Alaskan malamutes are big but very friendly dogs.

The Dog for You?

Alaskan malamutes are big, beautiful animals. They are powerful and fun-loving dogs.

Malamutes are unusually friendly, both with their owners and strangers. Don't approach a malamute if you're not prepared for a slurpy kiss.

Malamutes are full of energy, so they require plenty of exercise. They like long walks, runs, or the chance to pull a sled. Malamutes can be kept indoors, but they still need plenty of exercise time outdoors.

Malamutes in the same pack or household usually enjoy each other's company, although males sometimes fight.

The first malamute pups were raised by Mahlemut people of Alaska.

Malamutes are independent by nature. They can be taught **obedience** commands, but they are not among the easiest breeds to teach.

Despite their friendliness toward people, malamutes can be aggressive toward livestock or other dogs. Malamutes may also be quick to bound off if they are not in a fenced yard or on-leash.

Malamutes need grooming at least once a week. During periods when they shed, more grooming is needed.

Malamutes love to howl, especially in a chorus with their own kind. On a snowy night, their howls stir up memories of their wild ancestors.

Warm as toast, malamute pups get ready to doze in a bed of snow.

Purebred malamutes like this one were in danger of disappearing in the early 1900s.

Malamutes of the Past

No one knows how Arctic people developed the first malamutes. However, these dogs certainly have a close relationship to wolves.

Outsiders first discovered malamutes in the 1700s. The dogs were owned by the Mahlemut people on Alaska's northwest coast. Mahlemuts loved their dogs as workers, but they also loved them as companions.

In the late 1800s, gold hunters flooded into Alaska. They wanted more dogs for work and faster dogs for races. Many malamutes were **crossed** with other dogs. Pure malamutes were in danger of disappearing.

In the 1920s a dog owner in New England brought some pure malamutes out of Alaska

Sit! An obedience-trained malamute does exactly what it's told.

Admiral Byrd chose cold-loving malamutes for their ability to work in sub-zero weather.

and began raising them. People began to notice malamutes.

Admiral Richard E. Byrd took malamutes on his journey to the South Pole in 1933. By 1935, malamutes were accepted by the American Kennel Club as a pure breed.

Looks

Malamutes have a broad skull and a blunt **muzzle**. Their dark eyes may appear wolfish but kindly. Their ears are upright and triangle shaped.

Malamutes have a deep chest and a strong, slightly arched neck. They have a fluffy, curled tail.

A malamute shows the black cap, broad skull, and almond-shaped eyes of its breed.

A curled, bushy tail is typical of malamutes and other Arctic dog breeds.

The usual colors of malamutes are from light gray to black or some shade of brown. Malamutes always have white mixed with the darker colors. They generally have a "cap" or "mask" of white. All-white malamutes are unusual.

A Note about Dogs

Puppies are cute and cuddly, but only after serious thought should anybody buy one. Puppies grow up.

Choosing the right breed requires some homework. And remember that a dog will require more than love and patience. It will need healthy food, exercise, grooming, a warm, safe place in which to live, and medical care.

A dog can be your best friend, but you need to be its best friend, too.

For more information about buying and owning a dog, contact the American Kennel Club at http://www.akc.org/index.cfm or the Canadian Kennel Club at http://www.ckc.cal/.

Glossary

ancestor (AN SES tur) — an animal that at some past time was part of the modern animal's family

breeds (BREEDZ) — particular kinds of domestic animals within a larger, closely related group, such as the Alaskan malamute breed within the dog group

crossed (KROSD) — to have been mated with an animal of a different breed

muzzle (MUZ zul) — the nose and jaws of an animal; the snout

obedience (oh BEE dee uns) — the willingness to follow someone's direction or command; a pre-set training program for dogs

Index

Further Reading

Carroll, David L. *The ASPCA Complete Guide to Pet Care.* Plume, 2001
Fogle, Bruce. *The Dog Owner's Manual.* DK Publishing, 2003
LeKernec, Bill. *Alaskan Malamute.* TFH Publications, 1999

Website to Visit

Alaskan Malamute Club of America at www.alaskanmalamute.org

About the Author

Lynn M. Stone is the author of more than 400 children's books. He is a talented natural history photographer as well. Lynn, a former teacher, travels worldwide to photograph wildlife in its natural habitat.